© 2002 by Barbour Publishing, Inc.

ISBN 1-58660-447-3

Cover art © Artville

All Scripture quotations are taken from the King James Version of the Bible.

Published by Barbour Books, an imprint of Barbour Publishing, Inc., P.O. Box 719, Uhrichsville, Ohio 44683, www.barbourbooks.com

Member of the
Evangelical Christian
Publishers Association

Printed in China
5 4 3 2 1

SEASON'S GREETINGS

RACHEL QUILLIN

DayMaker
GREETING BOOKS

WE WISH YOU A MERRY CHRISTMAS

We wish you a Merry Christmas,
We wish you a Merry Christmas,
We wish you a Merry Christmas,
And a Happy New Year.

Good tidings to you,
And all of your kin,
Good tidings for Christmas,
And a Happy New Year.

MAY THE JOY OF
THAT FIRST CHRISTMAS
BE YOURS

I WILL HONOR CHRISTMAS IN MY HEART
AND TRY TO KEEP IT ALL THE YEAR.

CHARLES DICKENS

DEAR JESUS, thank You for coming to earth that first Christmas. Thank You for the new life and joy that we have because of Your great love. Help us to eagerly share it with others.

MY SOUL DOTH MAGNIFY THE LORD,
AND MY SPIRIT HATH REJOICED IN GOD MY SAVIOUR.

LUKE 1:46–47

CHRIST was born in the first century,
yet He belongs to all centuries.
He was born a Jew,
yet He belongs to all races.
He was born in Bethlehem,
yet He belongs to all countries.

GEORGE W. TRUETT

THE universal joy of Christmas is certainly wonderful. We ring the bells when princes are born, or toll a mournful dirge when great men pass away. Nations have their red-letter days, their carnivals and festivals, but once a year and only once, the whole world stands still to celebrate the advent of a life. Only Jesus of Nazareth claims this worldwide, undying remembrance. You cannot cut Christmas out of the calendar nor out of the heart of the world.

ANONYMOUS

Joy to the World

Joy to the world! the Lord is come!
Let earth receive her King;
Let every heart prepare Him room,
And heaven and nature sing,
And heaven and nature sing,
And heaven, and heaven, and nature sing.

Joy to the earth! the Savior reigns!
Let men their songs employ;
While fields and floods, rocks, hills, and plains
Repeat the sounding joy,
Repeat the sounding joy,
Repeat, repeat the sounding joy.

No more let sins and sorrows grow,
Nor thorns infest the ground;
He comes to make His blessings flow
Far as the curse is found,
Far as the curse is found,
Far as, far as the curse is found.

He rules the world with truth and grace,
And makes the nations prove
The glories of His righteousness,
And wonders of His love,
And wonders of His love,
And wonders, wonders of His love.

ISAAC WATTS

LOVE CAME DOWN AT CHRISTMAS

Love came down at Christmas,
Love all lovely, love divine;
Love was born at Christmas,
Star and angels gave the sign.

CHRISTINA ROSSETTI

WHEN THEY SAW THE STAR,
THEY REJOICED WITH EXCEEDING GREAT JOY.

MATTHEW 2:10

WISHING YOU GOD'S BLESSINGS AS YOU CELEBRATE OUR SAVIOR'S BIRTH

O HOLY NIGHT

O holy night, the stars are brightly shining;
It is the night of the dear Savior's birth!
Long lay the world in sin and error pining,
Till He appeared and the soul felt its worth.
A thrill of hope, the weary soul rejoices,
For yonder breaks a new and glorious morn.

Led by the light of faith serenely beaming,
With glowing hearts by His cradle we stand.
So led by light of a star sweetly gleaming,
Here came the wise men from Orient land.
The King of kings lay thus in lowly manger,
In all our trials born to be our friend!

Truly He taught us to love one another;
His law is love and His Gospel is peace.
Chains shall He break, for the slave is our brother,
And in His Name all oppression shall cease.
Sweet hymns of joy in grateful chorus raise we,
Let all within us praise His holy Name!
Fall on your knees, O hear the angel voices!
O night divine, O night when Christ was born!
O night, O holy night, O night divine!

TRANSLATED BY JOHN SULLIVAN DWIGHT

SEASON'S GREETINGS

AND, *behold, thou shalt conceive in thy womb, and bring forth a son, and shalt call his name JESUS.*

He shall be great, and shall be called the Son of the Highest: and the Lord God shall give unto him the throne of his father David:

And he shall reign over the house of Jacob for ever; and of his kingdom there shall be no end.

LUKE 1:31–33

TAKE time to be aware that in the very midst of our busy preparations for the celebration of Christ's birth in ancient Bethlehem, Christ is reborn in the Bethlehems of our homes and daily lives. Take time, slow down, be still, be awake to the Divine Mystery that looks so common and so ordinary yet is wondrously present.

EDWARD HAYS

THE *simple shepherds heard the voice of an angel*
and found their Lamb;
the wise men saw the light of a star
and found their wisdom.

FULTON J. SHEEN

BLESSED BE THE LORD GOD OF ISRAEL;
FOR HE HATH VISITED AND REDEEMED HIS PEOPLE,
AND HATH RAISED UP AN HORN OF SALVATION FOR US
IN THE HOUSE OF HIS SERVANT DAVID.

LUKE 1:68–69

AT Christmastime people seem ready to stop and acknowledge the blessings of God—more than at any other time of the year. After all, this is the time we've set aside to celebrate His greatest blessing to mankind—the gift of His perfect, holy Son, Jesus Christ. Only through Him can we truly enjoy the many gifts that God bestows upon us. So, as we celebrate this joyful season, let's take a moment; let's reflect upon the many times that God has blessed us this year. As we count our blessings, we may be surprised and delighted to discover that they are innumerable!

PRAYING
YOU'LL BE FILLED WITH
GOD'S PEACE AND LOVE
DURING THIS SPECIAL SEASON

DEAR GOD, please be with my loved ones at this wonderful time. There is so much excitement, and there are so many things to do. It's easy to become overwhelmed by the hectic schedules that we place upon ourselves. Lord, please keep each friend and family member in your care. Give everyone the peace that we can know only through You. Help us all to relax so that we might fully experience the joy of Christmas. Thank You.

AND THE ANGEL SAID UNTO THEM,
FEAR NOT: FOR, BEHOLD,
I BRING YOU GOOD TIDINGS OF GREAT JOY,
WHICH SHALL BE TO ALL PEOPLE.
FOR UNTO YOU IS BORN THIS DAY IN THE CITY OF DAVID
A SAVIOUR, WHICH IS CHRIST THE LORD.

LUKE 2:10–11

CHRISTMAS *is not a myth, not a tradition, not a dream. It is a glorious reality. It is a time of joy. Bethlehem's manger crib became the link that bound a lost world to a loving God. From that manger came a Man who not only taught us a new way of life but brought us into a new relationship with our Creator. Christmas means that God is interested in the affairs of people; that God loves us so much that He was willing to give His Son.*

BILLY GRAHAM

I HEARD THE BELLS ON CHRISTMAS DAY

I heard the bells on Christmas day
Their old familiar carols play,
And wild and sweet the words repeat
Of peace on earth, good-will to men!

And thought how, as the day had come,
The belfries of all Christendom
Had rolled along the unbroken song
Of peace on earth, good-will to men!

Till, ringing, singing on its way,
The world revolved from night to day,
A voice, a chime, a chant sublime
Of peace on earth, good-will to men!

And in despair I bowed my head;
"There is no peace on earth," I said;
"For hate is strong and mocks the song
Of peace on earth, good-will to men!"

Then pealed the bells more loud and deep:
"God is not dead, nor doth He sleep!
The wrong shall fail, the right prevail,
With peace on earth, good-will to men!"

HENRY W. LONGFELLOW

GLORY TO GOD IN THE HIGHEST,
AND ON EARTH PEACE, GOOD WILL TOWARD MEN.

LUKE 2:14

SOMEHOW, *not only at Christmas,*
but all the long year through,
the joy that you give to others
is the joy that comes back to you.

JOHN GREENLEAF WHITTIER

BUT when the fulness of the time was come,
God sent forth his Son, made of a woman, made under the law,
to redeem them that were under the law,
that we might receive the adoption of sons.

GALATIANS 4:4–5

22

GOD BLESS YOU
NOW AND ALWAYS

AND the angel came in unto her, and said,
Hail, thou that art highly favoured, the Lord is with thee:
blessed art thou among women.

LUKE 1:28

CHRISTMAS *is based on an exchange of gifts:*
the gift of God to man—His Son;
and the gift of man to God—
when we first give ourselves to God.

ANONYMOUS

IT WAS always said of him, that he knew how to keep Christmas
well, if any man alive possessed the knowledge. May that be truly
said of us, and all of us! And so, as Tiny Tim observed, "God
Bless Us, Every One!"

CHARLES DICKENS

GOD *grant you the light in Christmas, which is faith;*
the warmth of Christmas, which is love;
the radiance of Christmas, which is purity;
the righteousness of Christmas, which is justice;
the belief in Christmas, which is truth;
the all of Christmas, which is Christ.

WILDA ENGLISH

BEST of all, Christmas means a spirit of love,
a time when the love of God
and the love of our fellow men should
prevail over all hatred and bitterness,
a time when our thoughts and deeds and the spirit of our lives
manifest the presence of God.

ANONYMOUS

O FATHER, MAY THAT HOLY STAR
GROW EVERY YEAR MORE BRIGHT,
AND SEND ITS GLORIOUS BEAMS AFAR
TO FILL THE WORLD WITH LIGHT.

WILLIAM CULLEN BRYANT

ARE YOU WILLING TO BELIEVE THAT LOVE IS
THE STRONGEST THING IN THE WORLD—
STRONGER THAN HATE, STRONGER THAN EVIL,
STRONGER THAN DEATH—
AND THAT THE BLESSED LIFE WHICH BEGAN
IN BETHLEHEM NINETEEN HUNDRED YEARS AGO
IS THE IMAGE AND BRIGHTNESS OF THE ETERNAL LOVE?
THEN YOU CAN KEEP CHRISTMAS.

HENRY VAN DYKE

WHAT CAN I GIVE HIM,
POOR AS I AM?
IF I WERE A SHEPHERD, I WOULD BRING A LAMB;
IF I WERE A WISE MAN,
I WOULD DO MY PART;
YET WHAT CAN I GIVE HIM—
GIVE MY HEART.

CHRISTINA ROSSETTI

MAY YOU ENJOY
THIS CHRISTMAS WITH
WONDER AND
CHILDLIKE AWE

HEAP ON MORE WOOD!—THE WIND IS CHILL;
BUT LET IT WHISTLE AS IT WILL,
WE'LL KEEP OUR CHRISTMAS MERRY STILL.

SIR WALTER SCOTT

SUFFER little children,
and forbid them not,
to come unto me:
for of such is the kingdom of heaven.

MATTHEW 19:14

CHRISTMAS, CHILDREN, IS NOT A DATE.
IT IS A STATE OF MIND.

MARY ELLEN CHASE

HE *who has not Christmas in his heart*
will never find it under a tree.

ROY SMITH

CHRISTMAS IS THE DAY THAT
HOLDS ALL TIME TOGETHER.

ALEXANDER SMITH

JINGLE BELLS

Jingle bells, jingle bells,
jingle all the way!
O what fun it is to ride
In a one-horse open sleigh.

Dashing through the snow
In a one-horse open sleigh,
Over the fields we go,
Laughing all the way;
Bells on bob-tails ring,
Making spirits bright,
What fun it is to ride and sing
A sleighing song tonight.

Jingle bells, jingle bells,
jingle all the way!
O what fun it is to ride
In a one-horse open sleigh.

HAPPY, happy Christmas, that can win us back to
the delusions of our childhood days,
recall to the old man the pleasures of his youth,
and transport the traveler back to
his own fireside and quiet home!

CHARLES DICKENS

MOVING *between the legs of tables and of chairs, rising or falling,
grasping at kisses and toys, advancing boldly, sudden to take alarm,
retreating to the corner of arm and knee, eager to be reassured, taking
pleasure in the fragrant brilliance of the Christmas tree.*

T. S. ELIOT

A LITTLE boy and girl were singing their favorite Christmas carol in church the Sunday before Christmas. The boy concluded "Silent Night" with the words, "Sleep in heavenly beans."

"No," his sister corrected, "not beans, peas."

AND *they came with haste, and found Mary, and Joseph, and the babe lying in a manger.*

And when they had seen it, they made known abroad the saying which was told them concerning this child.

And all they that heard it wondered at those things which were told them by the shepherds.

LUKE 2:16–18

AT CHRISTMAS AND ALWAYS,
MAY YOUR HEART REJOICE
IN THE GIFTS OF GOD!

HOW GREAT OUR JOY

While by the sheep we watched at night,
Glad tidings brought an angel bright.
There shall be born, so he did say,
In Bethlehem a Child today.
There shall the Child lie in a stall,
This Child who shall redeem us all.
This gift of God we'll cherish well,
That ever joy our hearts shall fill.
How great our joy! Great our joy!
Joy, joy, joy! Joy, joy, joy!
Praise we the Lord in heaven on high!
Praise we the Lord in heaven on high!

Translated by THEODORE BAKER

THE rooms were very still while the pages were softly turned and the winter sunshine crept in to touch the bright heads and serious faces with a Christmas greeting.

LOUISA MAY ALCOTT

IT IS CHRISTMAS IN THE MANSION,
YULE-LOG FIRES AND SILKEN FROCKS;
IT IS CHRISTMAS IN THE COTTAGE,
MOTHER'S FILLING LITTLE SOCKS.
IT IS CHRISTMAS ON THE HIGHWAY,
IN THE THRONGING BUSY MART;
BUT THE DEAREST, TRUEST CHRISTMAS
IS THE CHRISTMAS IN THE HEART.

ANONYMOUS

BUT the angel said unto him,
Fear not, Zacharias: for thy prayer is heard;
and thy wife Elisabeth shall bear thee a son,
and thou shalt call his name John.
And thou shalt have joy and gladness;
and many shall rejoice at his birth.

LUKE 1:13–14

DEAR LORD, *as Zacharias and Elisabeth rejoiced for the birth of their own son that first Christmas, may we also rejoice in Your many blessings to us. Thank You, God, for these blessings. Please help us to share them with others. Amen.*

REFLECTIVE JOY

I FEEL the influence of the season beaming into my soul from the happy looks of those around me. Surely happiness is reflective like the light of heaven; and every countenance, bright with smiles and glowing with innocent enjoyment, is a mirror, transmitting to others the rays of a supreme and ever-shining benevolence.

WASHINGTON IRVING

THEN BE YE GLAD, GOOD PEOPLE,
THIS NIGHT OF ALL THE YEAR,
AND LIGHT YE UP YOUR CANDLES;
HIS STAR IS SHINING NEAR!

AUTHOR UNKNOWN

AND *the ransomed of the Lord shall return,*
and come to Zion with songs and everlasting joy upon their heads:
they shall obtain joy and gladness.

ISAIAH 35:10

A MERRY CHRISTMAS TO EVERYBODY!
A HAPPY NEW YEAR TO ALL THE WORLD!

CHARLES DICKENS